Yellow Umbrella Books are published by Capstone Press
151 Good Counsel Drive, P.O. Box 669, Mankato, Minnesota 56002
www.capstonepress.com

Library of Congress Cataloging-in-Publication Data
VanVoorst, Jennifer, 1972–
    Can you guess? / by Jennifer VanVoorst.
    p. cm.
    Summary: Simple text and photographs introduce the concept of estimation.
    ISBN 0-7368-2931-8 (hardcover)—ISBN 0-7368-2890-7 (softcover)
    1. Estimation theory—Juvenile literature. [1. Estimation theory.] I. Title.
QA276.8.V34 2004
519.5′44—dc22   2003011914

Editorial Credits
Editorial Director: Mary Lindeen
Editor: Jennifer VanVoorst
Photo Researcher: Wanda Winch
Developer: Raindrop Publishing

Photo Credits
Cover: BananaStock; Title Page: Corel; Page 2: EyeWire; Page 3: Royalty-Free/Corbis;
Page 4: PhotoLink/Photodisc; Page 5: Andersen Ross/Photodisc; Page 6: elektraVision/
Image Source; Page 7: Ryan McVay/Photodisc; Page 8: LWA-JDC/ Corbis; Page 9:
Jim Craigmyle/Corbis; Page 10: David Buffington/Photodisc; Page 11: Stockbyte;
Page 12: EyeWire; Page 13: BananaStock; Page 14: elektraVision/Image Source; Page 15:
Louis K. Meisel Gallery/Corbis; Page 16: elektraVision/Image Source

Can You Guess?

by Jennifer VanVoorst

Consultants: David Olson, Director of Undergraduate Studies, and Tamara Olson, PhD, Associate Professor, Department of Mathematical Sciences, Michigan Technological University

Yellow Umbrella Books

an imprint of Capstone Press
Mankato, Minnesota

Measuring

You measure things every day.
Sometimes you need to
measure exactly.

When you build, you need to measure exactly.

Estimating

Other times a close answer can be good enough.
You can make a guess.

You can guess the temperature by feeling the air outside.

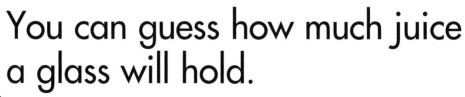

You can guess how much juice
a glass will hold.

When you make a guess, you estimate. You use what you know or can see to make a guess without counting or measuring.

Estimating Time

There are many things you can estimate. You can estimate time.

Here comes the bus.
Can you guess what time it is?

Your stomach is growling.
Can you guess how much
longer until lunch?

The sun is setting. Can you guess how much more time you have to play outside?

Estimating Amount

You can also estimate an amount.

You might estimate how much food will fit on your plate or in your stomach.

How do you know how much
milk to pour on your cereal?
Do you measure or guess?

Let's estimate! This gumball machine has 60 gumballs in it. Can you guess how many more gumballs it can hold?

Estimating is fast and fun!
When do you estimate?
Can you guess?

Words to Know/Index

Word Count: 196
Early-Intervention Level: 15